Little Marie's Life in Jamaica

Written By: Olivia Parks-May

To Norenha family. Love Olivia Paalk-May

Dear Reader:

Never give up on your dreams.
When I was little girl, I dreamt
of writing poems and books.
Today, my dream has come true.
Someday, your dream will come
true too.
Sincerely;

Olivia Parks-May

ISBN # 979–8–9856011 – 0–7

Dedication

This book is dedicated to
Jesus Christ my Lord and Savior.
To you be all the glory and honor.
Thank you for giving me the vision for this book.
To my loving husband Christopher: Thank you for
your total love & support.
To my four children: Daniella, Christopher, Gabriel
and Israel. You all are the joy and light of my life.
To my grandparents Sigeman & Madgerine Minott,
Wilford & Freida Hayres and Selvin Lambert. Thank
you all for your collective love and awesome family
memories.
To my parents Anthony & Lillieth Lambert-Grant.
Thank you for your love and teaching me that I could
do and be anyone I choose to through hard work.

Little Marie's Life in Jamaica

Written by Olivia Parks-May

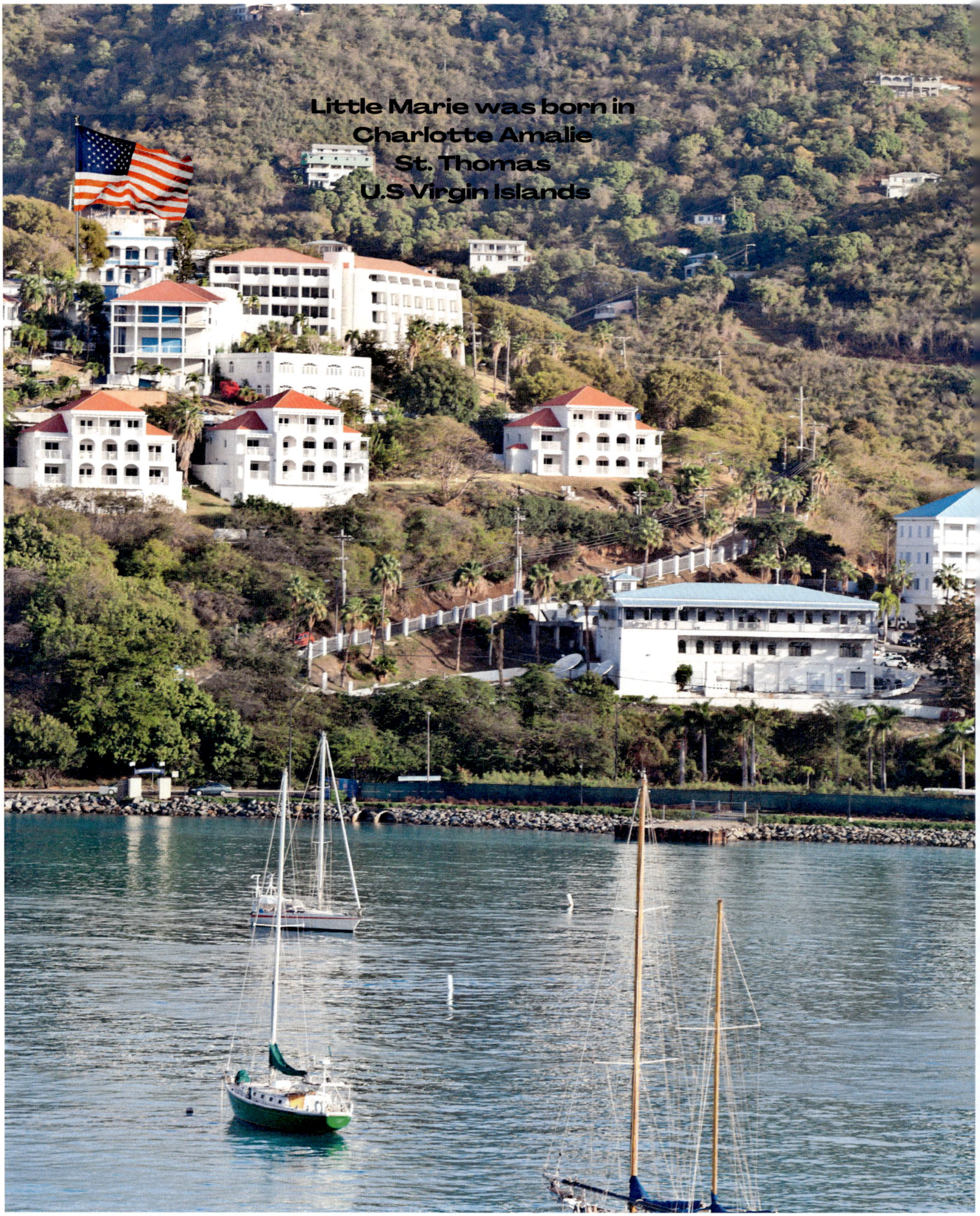
Little Marie was born in
Charlotte Amalie
St. Thomas
U.S Virgin Islands

Marie and her mother moved to Jamaica, West Indies when Marie was a baby.
Her & her mom flew to Jamaica in an airplane.
When they arrived, they lived in the capital of Kingston with her grandparents Wilford & Freida Hayres & many aunts & uncles.

ONE
LOVE

Life in the City

Marie was an only child and had a big family with three sets of grand parents: Grandma & grandpa Hayres, grandpa Lambert & Grandma & grandpa Minott. Marie had lots of aunts, uncles & cousins. They lived in two large family homes. One family farm home in the country, was located in Lindos Gap, St. Andrews & the other family home was in the city, located in the capital of Kingston.

Marie enjoyed climbing her favorite mango tree at their city home. She loved this mango tree because, she would sit under its branches on the roof top of their veranda, and eat delicious and juicy mangoes after school.

On Saturday afternoons; after she had finished her chores. She would spend hours in her favorite spot. There she could hear reggae music coming from several of the neighbors' houses. She read books, colored pictures and watched her neighbors while they washed and hung their clothes, to dry on clothes lines, swept their yards with straw brooms, and watched some of the neighborhood children playing.

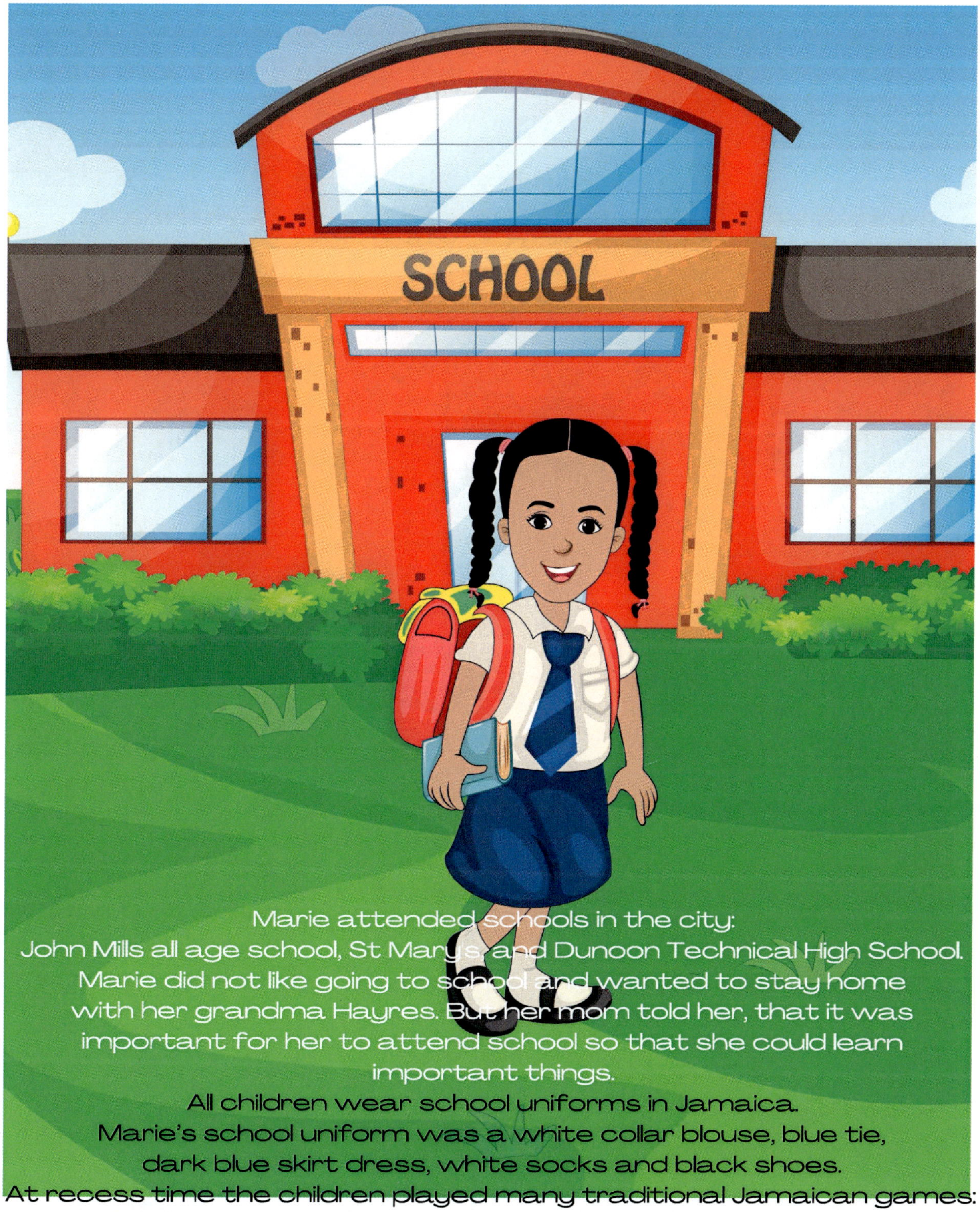

Marie attended schools in the city:
John Mills all age school, St Mary's, and Dunoon Technical High School.
Marie did not like going to school and wanted to stay home with her grandma Hayres. But her mom told her, that it was important for her to attend school so that she could learn important things.
All children wear school uniforms in Jamaica.
Marie's school uniform was a white collar blouse, blue tie, dark blue skirt dress, white socks and black shoes.
At recess time the children played many traditional Jamaican games: netball, jump rope, relay races, Dandi Shandi and Mother May I.
Marie's two favorite games to play at recess were: Dandi Shandi and Mother May I..

A day at the beach

Marie's mother worked as a passenger bus driver. She promised to take Marie and her aunt Sherine to the beach on her next day off. The day finally came for their trip to the beach and the girls were over the moon with excitement. They were packed and ready for their fun day at the beach.
They took two big passenger buses to get to the beach.

When they arrived at the beach, the water was a beautiful aqua blue color, the soft breeze coming off the Caribbean Sea felt like a million butterfly kisses, all at once. Marie really loved being at the beach. She was so happy and wished she could stay there for a really long time. The girls frolicked and played in the salty water and white sand: They gathered star fish, sea urchins & seashells.
They ran on the beach with their arms stretched out wide, pretending they were flying.
The girl's giggled as they took turns burying each others' legs and arms in the white sand. While Marie's mom watched them from nearby. She had a newspaper she was reading, but would glance up from it every few minutes, to kept an eye on the girls. Soon, It was lunchtime and the girls little tummies began to grumble from hunger. "Mommy what's for lunch?" Asked Marie. "We will have festivals, fried fish & coconut water from the seaside vendor," replied her mom.

"Yeah!" The girls squealed and ran towards the seaside vendor.

Lunch was so yummy and the girls ate until their little tummies were full. After lunch they returned to play on the beach and in the water. Later, Marie's mom called: "Girls it's 4:30 p.m. and it's time for us to go back home." Marie, looked at her aunt Sherine and then looked at her mom and said: "Already mommy?" Marie's mom replied: "Yes, it's time for us to go." "Don't worry we will come back another time." "Okay," replied Marie and Sherine in unison.

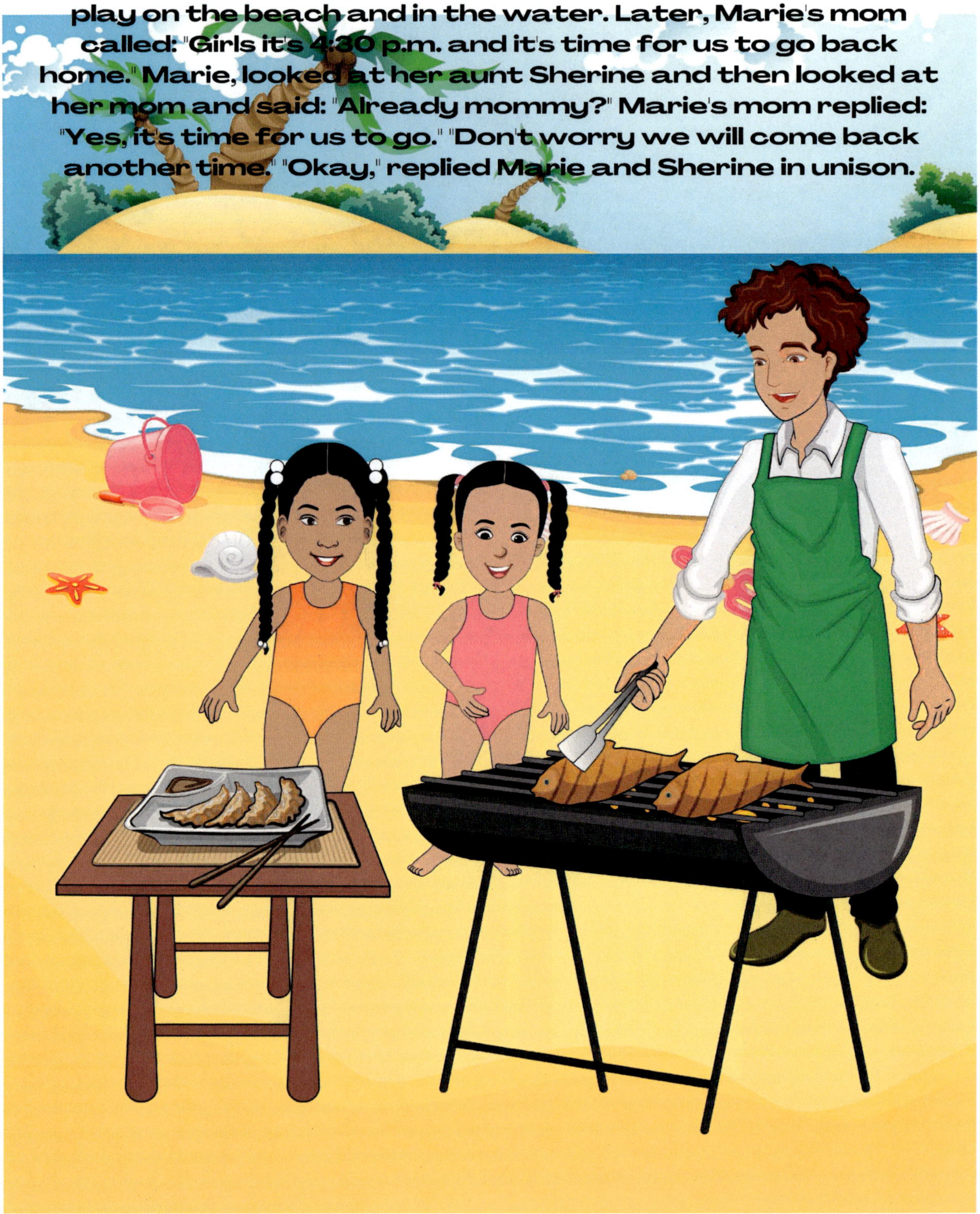

Sunday Special

Marie especially loved Sundays.
Sundays were Marie favorite day of week for two reasons: attending church with her grandmother Hayres and having family dinners. Her mom, grandmothers Minott & Hayres, all her aunts, uncles & cousins would get together for a family Sunday dinner. After dinner the entire family would either watch a sporting event or a family movie on the television in the living room.

Family Sunday Dinner

Country Life at her grandparents Minott's Farm

Marie would visit her grandmother Minott's farm during the summer time. Marie loved her visits to the farm because life on the farm was so much fun. She enjoyed getting on the big goats and cows' backs and chasing after the farm animals. Marie would chase the animals for hours. She also enjoyed feeding the chickens, pigeons and other animals. But, Marie was afraid of the pigs, they smelled bad and made scary sounds so she stayed away from them. She would help her grandma cook meals over an open fire and helped her in her garden too. Marie loved gardening with her grandmother and enjoyed learning all about herbs and flowers.

Her grandmother Minott knew a lot about plants and gardening.

During her visit with her grandmother, Marie enjoyed taking trips to a nearby river with her aunt Honey.

Marie and her aunt Honey were very close in age and they felt more like sisters rather than aunt and niece. Honey and Marie often went to the river on hot summer days. The girls would walk to the river together; there they had fun swimming and catching Janga (river shrimp). Marie was afraid of Janga because they looked funny & would mostly watch her aunt Honey catch them. Honey was very good at catching Janga.

Because Marie was a City girl, she had a difficult time learning to carry water in a water bucket on her head; no matter how many times she practiced carrying water on her head, she had a hard time doing it without spilling water all over her clothes.
Families in the country had to carry water from the river to their homes for cooking, washing dishes, washing clothes and other things; because there was no tap water for them to use.
On this day when the girls arrived from the river. Marie was soaking wet with the water from the water bucket on her head..

Grandma Minott met the girls in the front yard. Upon seeing Marie soaking wet, she busted into laughter.
"Neva mind mi darlin, yo try yo best," said grandma Minott as she took the bucket of water from Marie's head and lead her by the hand toward the house saying: "Go put sum dry clothes on now mi love."

Marie's Grandpa Minott was a farmer & he loved to laugh, sing traditional Jamaican songs and tell stories. When he laughed it was a real belly laugh and his laugh was loud too. Marie loved to hear her grandpa laugh. It was such a funny sight to see, and it always made Marie laugh too. Grandpa Minott was an amazing farmer; his fruits and vegetables were super big. Sometimes he would take Marie with him to the fields to gather crops, to sell at their farmers market on Saturday mornings. Marie would ride on the back of one of her grandpa's cows to the fields. Grandpa Minott would walk next to the cow all the way to and from the fields.

Grandpa Minott would sing:

There's a brown girl in the ring,

Tra la la, la. There's a brown girl in the ring, Tra la, la, la la. And she looks like a sugar on a plum, plum, plum!

Grandpa Lambert Marie's other grandpa lived close to her grandparents Minott's farm. Grandpa Lambert would visit them and always brought Marie Jamaican ice-cream, sky juice or bag juice and spending money.

Little Marie had a very happy life in beautiful Jamaica, surrounded by her very large family.

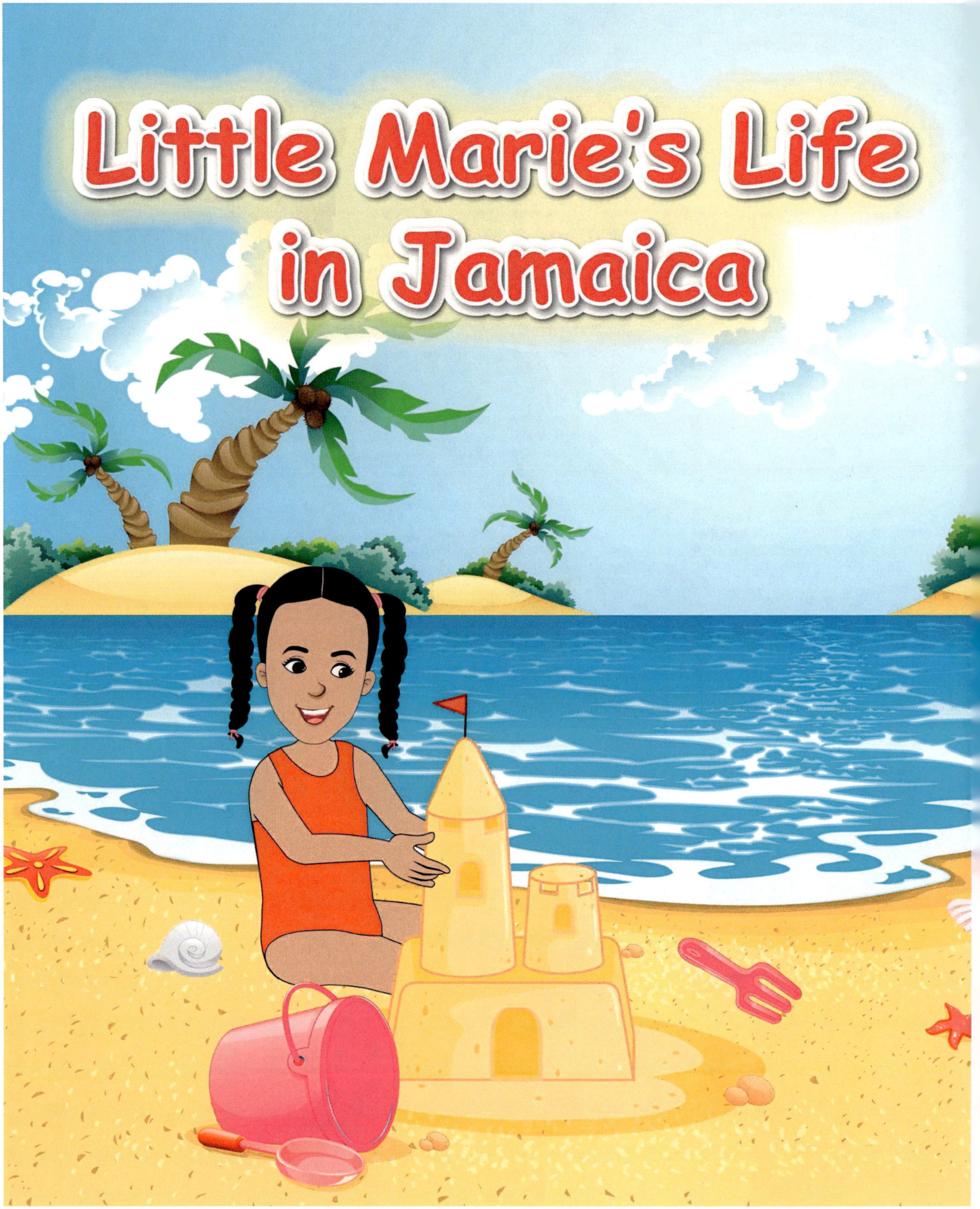
Little Marie's Life
in Jamaica

Made in the USA
Monee, IL
03 August 2022

10854949R00019